MW01627604

Dedications

To Julien (age 12) thanks for proof-reading this book and offering valuable insights to what a kid finds interesting. Thank you for your love of books, your interest in other cultures, and your brilliant sense of humour.

To Beau (age 8) for his love of fun facts and art. Beau has a deep love and respect for all living things; plants and animals alike. References to animals native to Belgium and details about the Cat Parade in Ypres were included in this book for Beau and all animal lovers.

"How can you not love a country famous for chocolate?" - Julien

LEARN ABOUT BELGIUM

For Kids

This Book Belongs to:

____

Learn About Belgium Contents

Learn About Belgium Contents

Where is Belgium?

Belgium is in Western Europe. It borders four other countries: The Netherlands, Germany, Luxembourg and France. A small part of Belgium has a coastline on the North Sea.

Fun Fact: Luxembourg used to be one country, but in 1839, the western part became a French province in Belgium, and the eastern part became its own country. Both the Belgian province and the country kept the name Luxembourg.

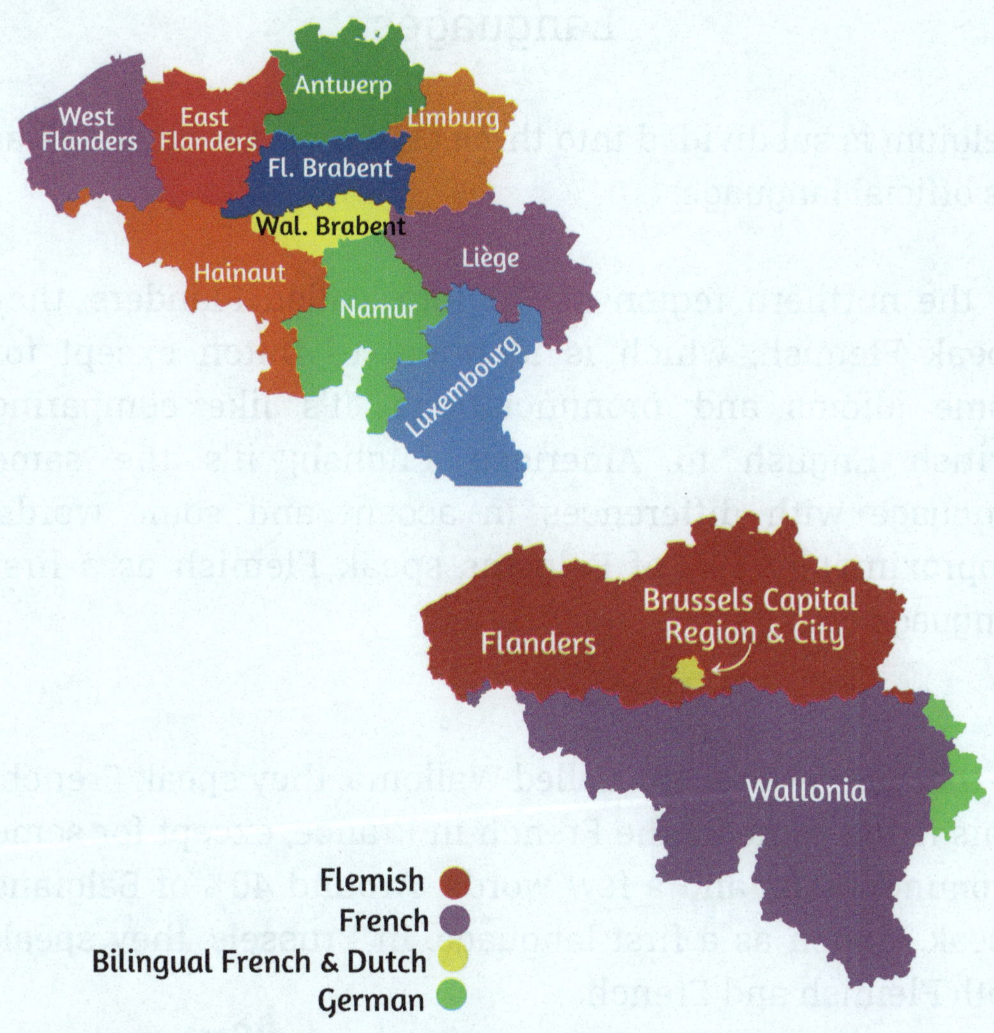

Belgium is divided into three regions and ten provinces.

The regions are Flanders, Wallonia and Brussels. Flanders and Wallonia each have five provinces. Brussels is unique because regional and provincial functions belong to a single capital region.

When you turn to the next page, titled "Languages," you'll learn that Belgium has three official languages, each spoken in a particular area of the country. The above map shows where these languages are spoken.

Languages

Belgium is subdivided into three states, and each state has its official language:

In the northern region of Belgium, called Flanders, they speak Flemish, which is identical to Dutch except for some idioms and pronunciations. It's like comparing British English to American English; it's the same language with differences in accent and some words. Approximately 59% of Belgians speak Flemish as a first language.

HALLO

In the southern region, called Wallonia, they speak French. This is the same as the French in France, except for some pronunciations and a few words. Around 40% of Belgians speak French as a first language. In Brussels, they speak both Flemish and French.

BONJOUR

In the small eastern region called Liége, they speak German. The German spoken there is identical to the language of Germany. About 1% of Belgians speak German as a first language.

GUTEN TAG

In addition to the three official languages, you can also hear regional dialects throughout the country, like Limburgish, Brabantian and East and West Flemish. There's also Low Dietsch, Walloon, Picard, Champenois and Lorrain.

How to Communicate in Belgium

With several official languages, none of them English, how should you communicate when travelling to Belgium?

You'll be glad that 55% of Belgians can speak English. But, if you know a bit of French or Dutch, try one of those languages first.

English	French	Dutch
Nice to meet you	Ravi de vous rencontrer	Aangenaam
Good bye	Au revoir	Tot ziens
Please	S'il vous plait	Alsjeblieft
How much does it cost?	Combien ça coûte?	Hoeveel kost het?
Excuse me	Excuse-moi	Pardon
How far is it?	A quelle distance est-ca?	Hoe ver is het?
Thank you	Merci	Bedankt
Where is ...	Où est ...	Waar is ...
Chocolate	Chocolat	Chocolade
Waffles	Gaufres	Wafels
Hello	Bonjour	Hallo

Money in Belgium

The currency in Belgium is the euro. Belgium moved from the Belgian franc to the euro on January 1, 2002. Today, twenty European countries use the euro.

The euro's value can change throughout the year depending on complicated factors. But as of the writing of this book in 2023, one euro is equal to:

1.09 American dollars ($)
1.47 Canadian dollars ($)
0.88 British pounds (£)

The symbol for the euro looks like this:

 *exchange rates change daily. The examples on this page were estimated from June 2023

The Belgian Flag

It would be easy to confuse Belgium's flag with Germany's. Both use the exact same colours, except they are in a different order, and the stripes go different ways: Belgium's flag has vertical stripes, and Germany's is horizontal.

Fun Fact: The stripes on the Belgian flag used to be horizontal like Germany's, but in 1830, Belgium gained independence from the Kingdom of the Netherlands and decided to flip the stripes to have a more unique flag of their own.

German Flag

The three colours in Belgium's flag have specific meanings:

Black = Humility
Yellow = Riches and Good Fortune
Red = Victory

The Weather in Belgium

Belgium has a **temperate maritime** climate, meaning moderate temperatures, with a lot of cloud cover and lots of rain.

Summer can be cool in Belgium. July and August get an average temperature of 20 - 25° C (68 - 77° F). Winter can be described as wet and chilly, with an average temperature between November and March of 3 - 7° C (37.4 - 44.6° F).

On average, Belgium gets more rainfall than the United Kingdom. The rainiest months in Belgium are July and December.

So what's the best time to visit Belgium for nice weather? There are five months the weather is its very best: April, May, June, September and October.

Storms and Natural Disasters

In February 2022, the worst storm in thirty years hit Belgium. Storm Eunice caused some property damage, downed trees and shut down schools and trains for the day. Storm Eunice killed 16 people across Europe, including Belgium.

Besides the occasional bad storm, Belgium is pretty safe from natural disasters.

The Population of Belgium

Over 11.697 million people live in Belgium.

The median age in Belgium is 41.9 years. This means half the population of Belgium is older than 41.9, and half are younger.

Population Density

Population density refers to the number of people living within one square kilometre (km) by dividing a country's total population by total land area.

Let's compare countries:

Country	Population Density per sq. km.
United States	37
United Kingdom	279
Bangladesh	1,315
Denmark	147
Australia	3
Belgium	383
Germany	239
Italy	200
France	118
Spain	95
Mexico	66
Singapore	8,323
Iceland	4
Canada	4

The population density in Belgium is 383 people per square kilometre. The chart above shows that Belgium is much more crowded than the United Kingdom and Germany. But remember, this is the average for the entire country, including big cities and the countryside.

Is your country on the list?

A Brief History of Belgium

1830: Belgium became a country by declaring independence from the Netherlands.

1831: The Kingdom of Belgium becomes a constitutional parliamentary monarchy. This means they elect a government and have a royal family like the UK.

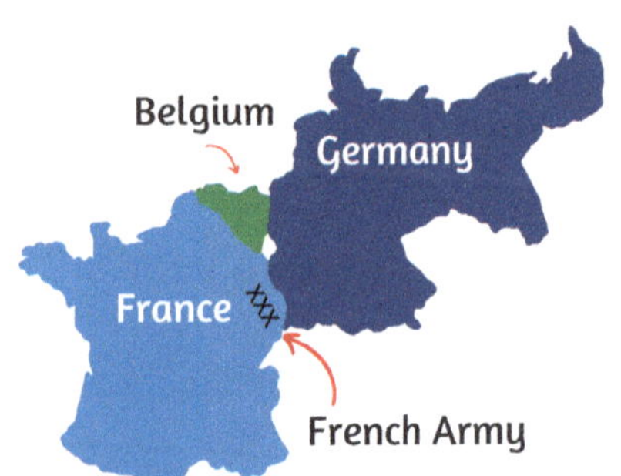

1914: Germany declared war on France (World War I). To avoid the French fortifications, Germany invaded Belgium so they could attack from there.

1917: Americans and Canadians entered the war in France but sent four armies who fought alongside the United Kingdom to help Belgium. The site of the battles happened in Flanders, and they named the area Flanders Fields. The famous war poem "Flanders Fields" spoke about the poppies there. From then on, the poppy became the symbol of Remembrance Day to honour our war heroes.

Fun Fact: Flanders Fields was written by Canadian army doctor, John McCrae.

A Brief History of Belgium

The Citizen
PEACE!
WORLD WAR ENDS; ARMISTICE SIGNED; KAISER IS OUT; REVOLUTION GROWS
ARMISTICE WILL TAKE EFFECT AT SIX A.M. TODAY
"PEOPLE'S GOVERNMENT" ESTABLISHED IN BERLIN APPEARS TO HAVE TRIUMPHED

1918: On November 11 (now Remembrance Day or Armistice Day), Germany was defeated, and Belgium got its country back.

1940 - 1944: World War II. Germany attacked Belgium again, and Belgium surrendered. Until the Western Allies rescued them, and Belgium was freed again.

1949: Belgium became one of the 12 countries and founding members of NATO (North Atlantic Treaty Organisation). Since then, 19 other countries have joined.

A Brief History of Belgium

1957: Belgium was one of the founding members of the European Economic Community (EEC), which later became the European Union (EU). The EU Headquarters is in Brussels.

1960: Belgium granted independence to its former colony, the Democratic Republic of the Congo (now known as the Republic of the Congo). Belgian King Leopold II had seized the African country in 1885 as his own personal possession!

1993: Belgium underwent a major political transformation and became a federal state with three regions: Flanders, Wallonia, and Brussels (see map on page 2)

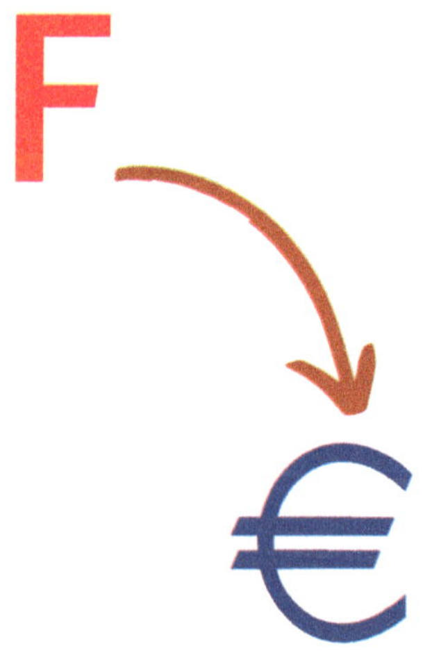

1999: Belgium adopted the euro as its currency, replacing the Belgian franc entirely by 2002. (see more on page 5)

A Brief History of Belgium

2003: Belgium promised to get rid of its seven nuclear reactors by 2025 in favour of renewable energy sources and gas.

Update: As of 2023, there are still five reactors left, and because Russia invaded Ukraine, Belgium has decided to extend the deadline by ten years for two of its power plants.

2010 - 2011: Belgium went 541 days without a government. This was the longest time any country has gone without an elected government. During this time, the former Prime Minister Yves Leterme served as caretaker.

How is School Different in Belgium?

- Children between 6 and 18 must attend school or receive at-home education.
- Primary school is for children ages 6-12.
- There are two types of primary schools: public schools and private schools. Public schools are free.
- Montessori and Waldorf are popular types of private schools in Belgium. Other types of alternative schools focus on student-led education.

This is a Freinet school in Belgium - a specific type of private school that allows the student to determine their learning pace. Students are considered co-workers alongside their teachers and have a meaningful say in how they are taught. Freinet schools are becoming more popular in many countries.

Homeschooling

Homeschooling is permitted in Belgium and has become more popular in recent years.

The Belgian government requires each homeschooled child to follow a specific curriculum and pass a yearly test. If the child fails, they may be required to attend a formal school.

Homeschool parents must sign a document agreeing to respect the UN Convention on Children's Rights. Parents must agree to provide education that includes the development of a child's personality and skills—respect for fundamental human rights for all.

Waffle Iron Politics and the Ghost Metro

As we mentioned on page 2, Belgium is divided into three regions: Flanders, Wallonia and Brussels. Brussels is the capital, making most of the country's big decisions.

Think of Belgium as a small family. Brussels is the parent, and Flanders and Wallonia are the kids. Brussels used waffle-iron politics to ensure they treated both kids fairly and did not give them a reason to fight. As you can see from the picture of the waffle iron, both sides are equal.

This sounds like a good idea, but it all fell apart when Brussels decided to give the kids an equal amount of money so they could build a metro (subway) in their two biggest cities.

The problem was that Liège in Wallonia and Ghent in Flanders didn't want to build a metro. So, again, to be fair, Brussels gave the excess money to the city in each region that still wanted a metro: Antwerp in Flanders and Charleroi in Wallonia. Even though Antwerp had twice the population as Charleroi, they both had equal money to build their metros.

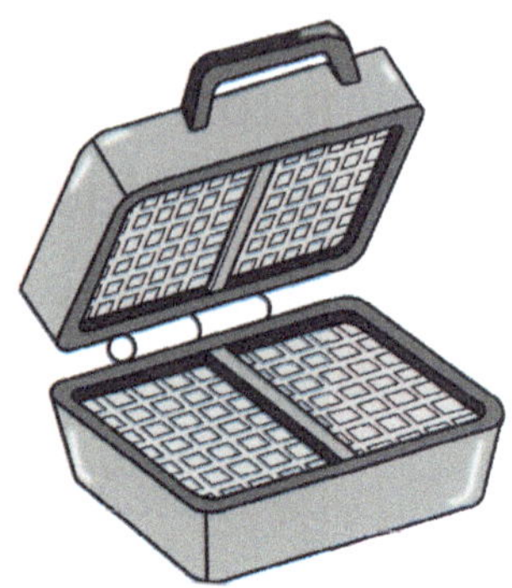

Having a population of about 400,000, Charleroi decided to go ahead and build eight lines (enough to service a million people!). But before they were finished, a new government came into power, removing the waffle-iron politics in 1988. Instead, Brussels gave more power to Wallonia and Flanders so they could spend their budgets how they wanted.

Now, the region of Wallonia said, "Whoa! We can't spend all that money on a metro for little Charleroi". So even though some stations were built entirely, with tracks and platforms and ticket offices and escalators, they never opened. Over the years, these ghost metro stations became overgrown with weeds and littered with graffiti.

But all is not lost! The metro in Charleroi was eventually funded and is expecting completion in 2026.

To clarify, Charleroi and Antwerp have what they call a metro; they are trams or LRTs (light rail transit), unlike Brussels, which has an actual metro.

Getting Around in Belgium

Today, getting around Belgium is fast and efficient, whether you take a tram or metro within the city,

Metro station in Brussels

Tram in Ghent

or a high-speed train to another city or a neighbouring country.

High-speed train leaving Brussels

Driving in Belgium

If you're travelling to Belgium, your parents may decide to rent a car or use a taxi or ride-share company.

In Belgium, they drive on the right side of the road, the same as in most countries. But if you're coming from the U.K., this will take some getting used to.

If you're taking taxis, using official black cars with a taxi light on the roof is important. They are also identified by the T in the licence plate. One warning: Belgian taxis are the most expensive in Europe.

Buses are also a convenient way to get around. Belgium has three bus companies: De Lijn, TEC and STIB.

The Landscapes of Belgium

Rolling Hills

Beaches and Waterfront

Forests

Modern Cities

Animals Native to Belgium

Wild Boar

Red Fox

Red Deer

Badger

Flemish Giant Rabbit

Wolf

Ermine

Pine Marten

The Story of Leo Belgicus

The Leo Belgicus, or the Lion of Belgium, was initially drawn as a map of Belgium in 1611.

The lion symbolised strength and courage, so the people of Belgium wanted this to represent their country. They wanted others to know that Belgians were strong and proud and would defend their country fiercely like a lion.

Today, Leo Belgicus is proudly displayed in the country's coat of arms and remains the symbol of Belgium.

Fun Fact: Through the centuries, the coat of arms has undergone many design changes, but since the 17th century, it has always included Leo.

Top Industries in Belgium

Steel

Textiles

Glass

Paper

Food Processing

Metal Processing and Refineries

Belgium is one of the world's leaders in processing metals and crude petroleum.

The provinces of East Flanders, Limburg and Hainaut, and the area between Antwerp and Brussels have the most manufacturing activity.

Where there are large manufacturers, there are lots of jobs, so these areas also see the largest population.

Top Exports

The top exports of Belgium (things they process and sell to other countries) are automobiles, medicines in dose form, and diamonds. Food grown or manufactured in Belgium exported to other countries is pictured below.

Due to its location, Belgium imports certain foods and re-exports them to other European countries—for example, Belgium imports and exports bananas from the Caribbean throughout Europe.

Belgium's largest trading partners are Germany, the Netherlands and France. They sell to other countries worldwide, but these three customers make up almost half of everything Belgium sells.

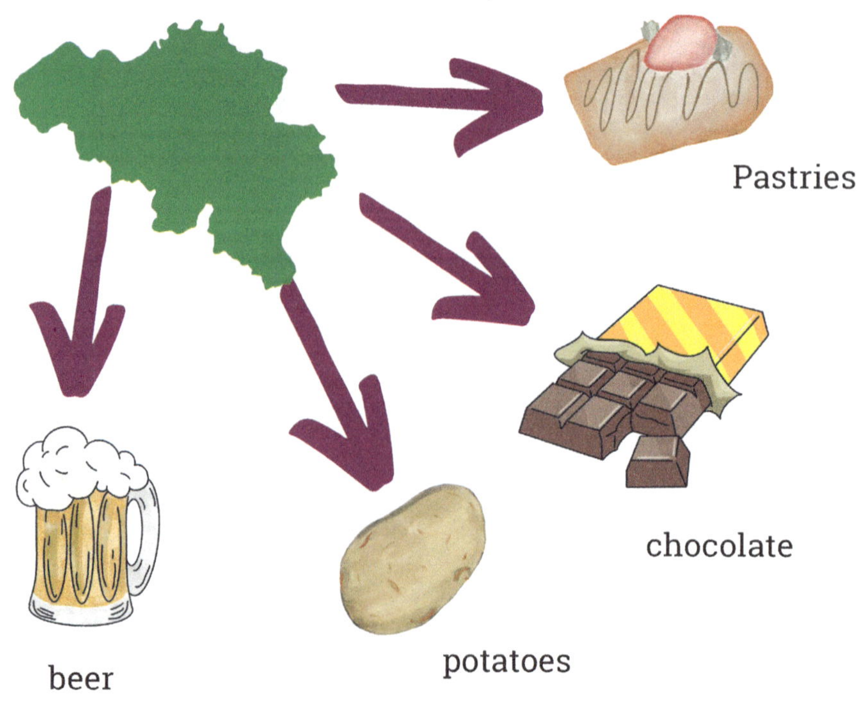

Top Imports

The top imports of Belgium (things they buy from other countries) include petroleum products, pharmaceuticals and automobiles.

Belgium is the world's third-largest importer of pharmaceuticals and number one for clinical trials. A clinical trial studies and tests new medicine.

During COVID, Belgium produced a significant supply of vaccines for Pfizer and AstraZeneca.

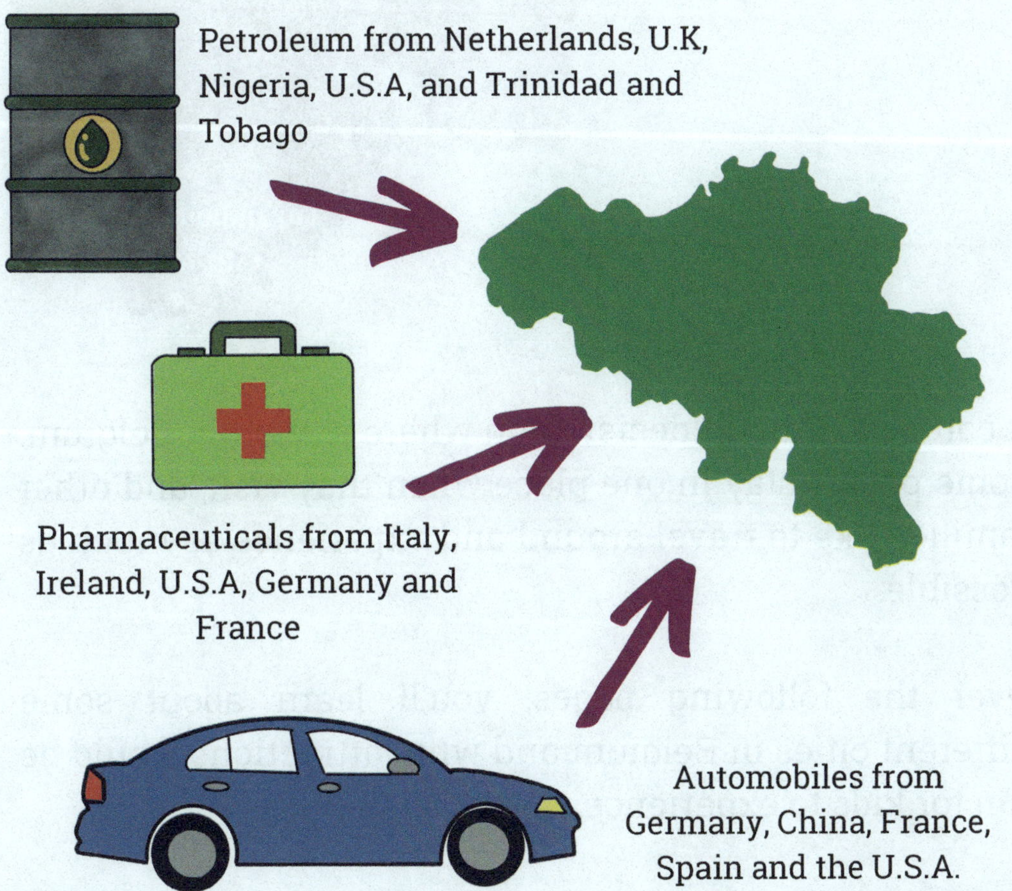

Most Popular Tourist Destinations

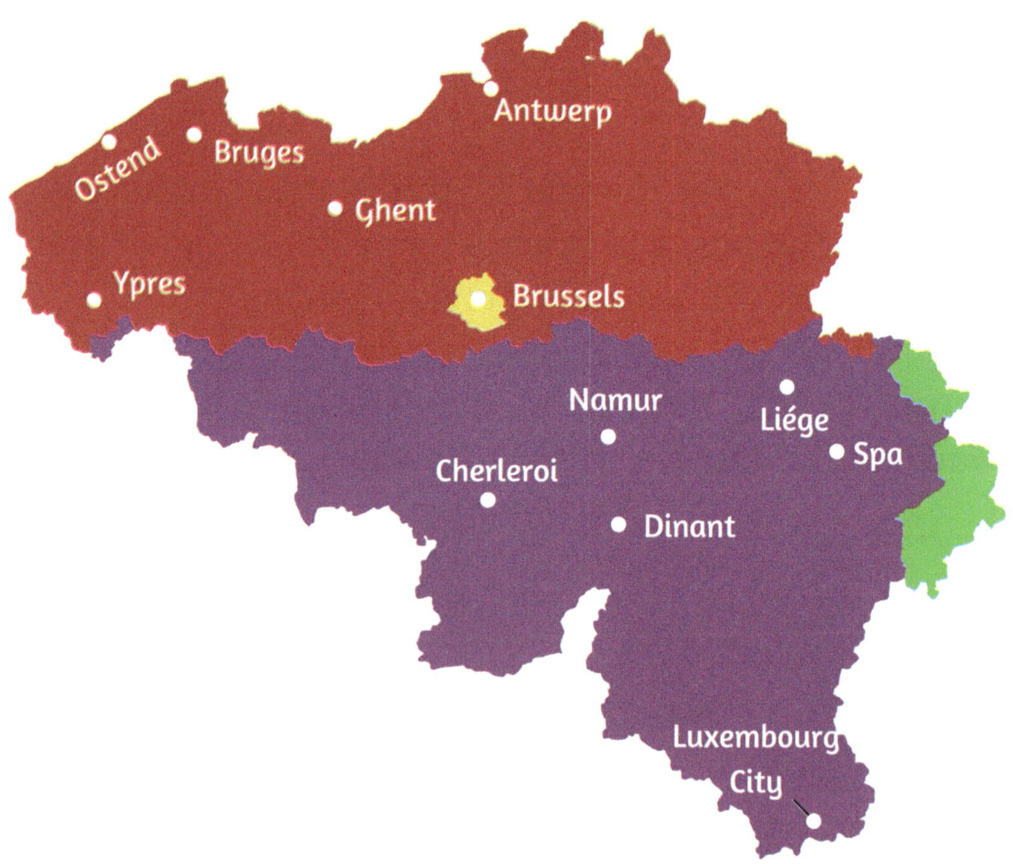

It can be a difficult decision on where to visit in Belgium. Some people stay in one place when they visit, and other families like to travel around and experience as much as possible.

Over the following pages, you'll learn about some different cities in Belgium and what attractions would be fun for kids to experience.

Brussels

Brussels is Belgium's capital city, with more than two million people. That's almost as big as Houston, Texas, in the United States or Toronto, Ontario, Canada.

A global city, Brussels is also known as "the capital of Europe" because the European Union (EU) headquarters is located there. The EU is an organization that brings many European countries together to work on common goals, like protecting the environment, promoting human rights, and improving trade.

Brussels is also where NATO (North Atlantic Treaty Organisation) is headquartered. NATO is a strong alliance of European and North American countries that vow to protect each other in defence, security and crisis management.

But there's more to Brussels than politics:

Fun Fact: The airport in Brussels sells more chocolate than anywhere else in the world. They sell about two tons of chocolate every day!

Brussels

One of Belgium's most famous landmarks is **Atomium** in Brussels. Atomium is an interactive exploration centre for families to learn and enjoy culture and digital art. It was built for Expo '58 but remains 65 years later as a must-visit place in Brussels.

Shaped like a giant atom, you travel through the structure by walking through tunnels. Each tunnel has escalators and light and sound animations. The tunnels are what join the nine stainless steel spheres that are each 18m (59 feet) in diameter.

Directly next door to Atomium is **Mini Europe.** This is a theme park where you can walk like a giant through the cities of Europe. The walk is interactive, meaning you can push buttons and make things happen. Would you like to know what it was like when Mount Vesuvius in Italy erupted? Just press a button and watch!

Brussels

Fun Fact: Brussels is the home of the Smurfs! Created by Belgian artist Peyo, who came from Brussels. You'll see statues throughout the city. Brussels Airlines even decorated one of their planes with Smurfs.

Brussels is also the home of Tintin, which is another famous cartoon. You'll find these characters throughout the city. You can even visit the Tintin Museum.

Brussels is nicknamed the Comic Strip Capital, and you can walk on the Comic Strip Route to see incredible giant murals! See page 42 for details.

Bruges

Bruges is sometimes called "The Venice of the North". Bruges has canals winding through the city, just like Venice, Italy. Taking a **Canal Tour** is something most tourists like to do.

The tour is short (only about 30 minutes), so some companies also add a walking tour. There's a canal boat tour leaving about every 15 minutes between 10:00 a.m. and 5:00 p.m. You can't reserve a boat tour, but five companies offer rides from March to November, so show up, buy a ticket, and get in line.

Remember to say hallo (hello) to the swans!

Bruges

Can you climb 366 steps? Then you'll enjoy the **Belfry Tower.** This is a medieval tower in the centre of Bruges. You'll get a fantastic view of the city from the top, and enjoy a cool museum too!

The tower was built in 1486 to store municipal archives and was the treasury office. They also used the tower as a post for spotting fires and other dangers.

Choco-Story: If you want to know all about the history of chocolate and how it's made, then this museum is for you! You can wander through and see almost a thousand unique chocolate-related objects. And once you're done, you get to taste some made right there in front of you.

Fun Fact: The history of chocolate goes back 4,000 years! Read more about chocolate on page 58.

Bruges

You may know by now that Belgium is famous for waffles and chocolate, but did you know that french fries were invented in Belgium? So you're probably asking why they are called "french" fries. It's because cutting food so that all sides are even for frying is called "frenching." So, the name refers to how they were cut (frenched fries), not where they came from.

This famous food was invented in Namur, but we mention it here because Bruges is the only place in the world with a french fry museum. It's called **Frietmuseum.** Learn more about french fries on page 57.

Finally, an excellent place for kids to explore in Bruges is **Historium Bruges**: This interactive museum takes you back to experience medieval Bruges. You can walk through recreated historical scenes and put on virtual reality headsets to see the city as it was centuries ago. You can even dress up in medieval costumes!

Antwerp

Fun Fact: Antwerp, Belgium, is the world's diamond capital and the second-largest port in Europe (more on page 44).

Plopsa Station Antwerp is a comic-themed indoor park in the Antwerp Central Station. It's dedicated to Belgian comic characters previously mentioned, along with even more. There are rides, interactive exhibits, and shows.

Antwerp

The Antwerp Zoo opened way back in 1843. It is one of the world's oldest zoos and is home to over 7,000 animals! Making it one of the largest and most diversified animal collections in Europe.

It is very close to Antwerp Central Station and Chocolate Nation.

There are chocolate museums and chocolate-making workshops all over Belgium. Still, **Chocolate Nation** is the world's largest Belgian Chocolate Museum, so we decided to focus on this one in Antwerp.

You will travel through 14 themed rooms and learn the entire history of chocolate, from the cocoa plantations in Ecuador to the largest cocoa storage port in Antwerp. Your 60-to 90-minute tour will take you through all the chocolate-making stages. And, of course, they will let you try some!

If you want to learn to make delicious chocolate, you can schedule a one-hour workshop that includes a museum tour and 200g (almost half a pound) of chocolates you made yourself to take home. Now that's an excellent souvenir!

Ghent

The best place to learn all about the City of Ghent and its history is **STAM, Ghent City Museum.** You'll be invited to sit on the floor and look at the city from the view of a giant overhead. Then, you can wander through fascinating exhibits throughout the museum.

Have you ever seen a castle with a moat? **Gravensteen Castle** is a medieval castle in Ghent built in 1180. It was once a house of torture! The idea can be very gruesome but also very interesting. If you're 12 or younger, it's free to get in.

Dinant

Dinant is a beautiful city in the Wallonia region of Belgium, where you'll find **Dinant Adventure Park.** If you like physical challenges, this is the place to go! You'll scale the side of a cliff, balance along scary rope bridges, and zipline your way across the park. You must be at least eight years old to go, and helmets are mandatory. And don't worry; you are attached to cables and carabiners the entire time.

You can't walk the streets of Dinant, without noticing all the giant saxophones, there are 60! Each one is decorated by representatives of countries throughout Europe. Why so many saxophones? The inventor of the saxophone was Adolphe Sax, who was born in Dinant. They are very proud of him.

Liége & Spa

Liége-Bastogne-Liége is a famous bike race that is more than 100 years old. The race begins and ends in Liége, Wallonia, and is 258.5 km (160.6 miles) long. So, if you happen to be visiting in April, get a spot and cheer on the cyclists who come from all over the world to compete.

If you prefer to watch races on four wheels instead of two, you can travel just a bit south of Liége to Spa. The **Belgian Grand Prix** is held in Spa every summer and has been part of the Formula One World Championship since 1925.

Belgium's Comic Book Culture

If you're lucky enough to visit Belgium, you'll soon find comic book characters everywhere! The reason you'll see so many cartoons is that Belgium is the birthplace of the comic strip. Two of the most famous Belgian comic book characters are Tintin and the Smurfs.

Besides painted murals and museums, Belgium also has comic-book awards and festivals. The **Brussels Comic Con Festival** is held in September and is super fun. You can meet famous comic book artists, see awesome exhibitions, and even dress up as your favourite characters. It's when everyone celebrates the magic of comics, adults and kids alike.

Fun Fact: In 2022, the Belgian government placed a famous cartoon scene on each Kingdom of Belgium's official passport page.

Comic Book Route - Brussels

There are more than 70 cartoon murals all over Brussels. If your family decides to complete the Comic Book Route walking tour, you can buy an official map at the Brussels Tourism Office for just one euro. Plan to spend three or four hours to complete the walk.

Lace Making - Bruges

Did you ever wonder how lace was made? Today, machines create pre-loaded patterns, but handmade lace is a proper art form. Some consider Bruges to be the lace capital of the world. If you know someone who sews beautiful things, you could pick the perfect piece of handmade lace for them as a thoughtful souvenir.

Lace Making School - 1920

Fun Fact: At one time, long ago, 25% of all the women in Bruges were lace-makers.

Diamonds in Antwerp

Fun Fact: About 85% of all the natural diamonds in the world have visited Antwerp.

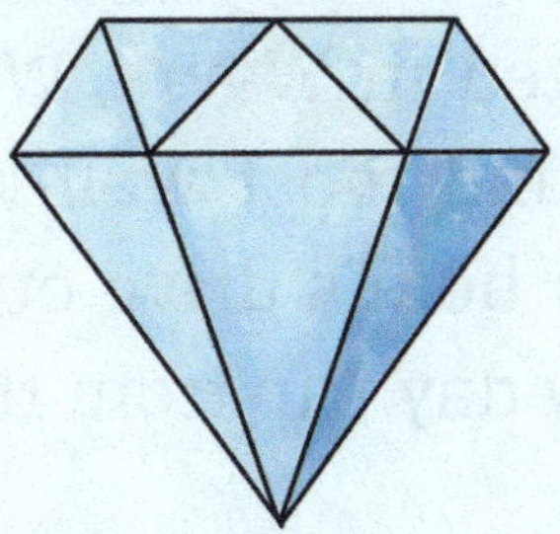

Antwerp is the home of the world's best diamond cutters. And if a diamond is certified there, it is a quality jewel.

Since the 14th century, the diamond trade has been centred in Antwerp. Buyers and sellers from all over the world come to this city to do business. They call the area the Diamond Exchange.

Since Antwerp has an impeccable reputation, having rough diamonds cut and polished in Antwerp means they are of the highest quality. Many countries try to compete, but many believe only the best diamonds are Antwerp diamonds. This has to do with the city's reputation for the highest craftsmanship and for its honesty in rating a diamond's quality and assessing its value.

Fun Fact: Diamonds are rated by type (natural or lab-grown), weight, shape, clarity, colour, and symmetry.

Belgian Theme Parks

We've already mentioned a couple of theme parks, but here are a few more:

Walibi Belgium: Located in Wavre, Walibi Belgium is one of Belgium's largest and most well-known theme parks. Wavre is less than an hour's drive outside of Brussels, so it would make an easy day trip from the capital.

Walibi Belgium offers a variety of thrilling rides, including ten roller coasters. Next door is **Aqualibi**, an indoor water park open all year round.

Plopsaland De Panne is a popular theme park based on the television characters created by Studio 100. It has themed attractions, gentle rides, shows, indoor and outdoor playgrounds, and live performances. You can also take a boat trip through a gnome forest!

De Panne is a good day trip from Bruges because it is less than an hour's drive away.

Bellewaerde is the oldest theme park in Belgium. It opened in 1954 originally as a zoo and safari. In the 1980s, the park added thrilling rides to appeal to teenagers.

Located near Ypres, Bellewaerde is an excellent place to spend time and enjoy the 30 rides and 300 animals. You can take the Bengal Express, a train that lets you view lions, tigers and monkeys up close.

Planckendael is an animal park near Mechelen (between Brussels and Antwerp). You can attend animal feedings and watch penguins, monkeys, lemurs and many more animals from around the world.

You can also enjoy cool outdoor adventures like swings, slides and a treetop trek in the forest.

Famous Belgian Inventions

Body Mass Index (BMI)
Mathematician Lambert
Adolphe Quetelet

Saxaphone - Adolphe Sax
1846 (more on page 39)

Synthetic Plastic
Leo Henricus Baekeland
1909

Asphalt - Chemist
Edward de Smedt 1870

Inline Skates - Horologist
John Joseph Merlin 1760

Famous Belgian Inventions

Jpegs (a format for compressing image files) - Physicist and Mathemetician Baroness Ingrid Daubechies

World Wide Web - co-invented by British Computer Scientist Tim Berners-Lee and Belgian Informatics Engineer and Computer Scientist Robert Cailliau 1990

Stock Exchange - Began in the 14th century when Belgium negotiated trade with the Germans and Italians

French Fries - Villagers in Meuse Valley in the late 1600s (more on page 57)

Public Holidays and Observances

Most Belgians are Roman Catholic, so many holidays are based on the Christian religion.

Jan 1	New Year's Day
March or April (Depends on the Year)	Easter Sunday
Monday after Easter	Easter Monday
May 1	Labour Day
39 days after Easter Sunday (always a Thursday)	Ascension day
A Sunday in May or June (depends on the year)	Whit Sunday
A Monday in May or June (depends on the year)	Whit Monday
July 21	Belgian National Day
August 15	Assumption of Mary
November 1	All Saints Day
November 11	Armistice Day
December 25	Christmas

Belgian National Day and the Monarchy

Belgium is a Monarchy. This means there is a King or Queen and a Royal Family. But in Belgium, the Monarchy is mostly symbolic. That means they don't make laws or decide how the country is run. Instead, they do essential ceremonial tasks and help represent Belgium to the rest of the world. They're an important symbol of Belgium's history and identity.

Belgian National Day celebrates when Belgium's first King, Leopold I, took the oath of office on July 21, 1831.

As of 2023, the King of Belgium is King Philippe. He is the seventh King and the great-great-great-grandson of King Leopold I. Philippe's daughter, Elisabeth, is next in line to the throne and will be Belgium's first Queen.

To celebrate Belgian National Day, Brussels has a big military parade. The Belgian King and members of the royal family usually attend along with members of the armed forces, police and emergency services.

Each city in Belgium celebrates with their festivities, including a big fireworks display, concerts and entertainment.

Carnivals

Binche Carnival: The most famous carnival in Belgium, held in Binche. The main feature of this carnival is the Gilles, men dressed in elaborate costumes and masks, who throw oranges into the crowd.

Aalst Carnival: This carnival is known for its satirical floats, where local and international politicians and celebrities are humorously depicted. This three-day event before Lent begins features a parade of floats, a broom dance by the Gilles of Aalst, and the burning of a puppet in the main square on the last day, symbolizing the conclusion of the carnival and the beginning of Lent.

Stavelot Laetare: This carnival, held in Stavelot, features the Blancs Moussis, characters dressed in white robes with long red noses. Participants engage in pillow fights and throw confetti while parading around the town.

Carnivals

Malmedy Carnival (Cwarmê): An event that lasts four days from Sunday to Tuesday before Ash Wednesday. The participants are masked figures in traditional costumes parading in the streets while singing traditional songs.

Eupen Carnival: A four-day celebration held in the German-speaking region of Belgium. This carnival is known for its Kloatschelepper parade on Shrove Tuesday, which features hundreds of participants dressed in straw costumes.

Dunkirk Carnival: Although it is technically held in the French town of Dunkirk, many Belgians from the nearby region participate in this carnival, which originated from local fishermen's traditions. The carnival is known for its "fish throw," where attendees try to catch raw herring thrown from the town's belfry.

Christmas Traditions

Just like in many countries, Christmas is a big deal in Belgium. People get time off work and school, and families exchange gifts, attend church, and celebrate with a big meal.

But Belgium has some Christmas traditions that might be different from what you see in your country:

- Gifts are delivered on **December 6** (not Christmas Eve, like in other countries).
- Santa Claus is called **Sinterklaas** in Belgium.
- Sinterklaas does not use reindeer. Instead, he flies on a **white horse**.
- Sinterklaas has an assistant called ***Zwarte Piet** (Black Pete). Zwarte Piet goes down chimneys to deliver gifts to the shoes left by the fireplace while Sinterklaas waits on the roof with his horse.
- Sinterklaas dresses a bit differently from Santa Claus in North America. In Belgium, Sinterklaas looks more like a Catholic Bishop.

*Although Zwarte Piet is probably black from the soot in all those chimneys, many people want him to retire because it can be seen as offensive to the black community.

Christmas Traditions

Sinterklaas and Zwarte Piet

Some Christmas traditions in Belgium are similar to other countries around the world:

- They decorate their house with nativity scenes, Christmas trees, and lights.
- In addition to Sinterklaas' gifts on December 6, some Belgians also place gifts under the tree on Christmas Eve.
- Christmas Eve dinner usually includes a roast turkey, seafood or chicken, and a favourite: potato croquettes.

Belgium's Commitment to Reducing Single Use Plastic

Unrecycled plastic is one of the worst polluters of our environment. To help correct the problem, Belgium is taking measures to reduce the use of harmful plastics in their country.

Since January 2023, some plastic products are no longer allowed to be sold in Belgium (except for current stock on hand).

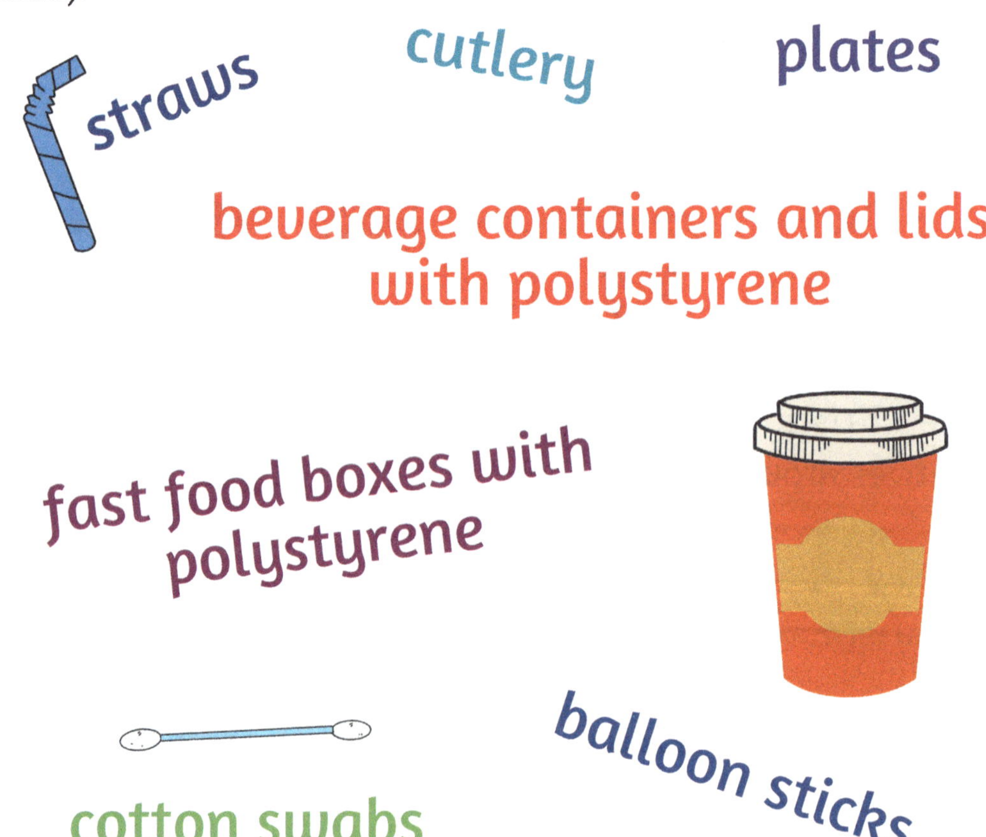

supermarket plastic bags

The Turtle Logo

Belgium, as with other countries in the European Union, requires using the Turtle Logo on any plastic products that are not yet banned but could harm the environment.

The logo reminds people that sea life (including turtles) is in danger because of the plastic in our oceans. It's the hope that when someone sees this label on a product they are using, they are reminded to recycle it responsibly.

Food in Belgium
French Fries

French fries (chips in the U.K.) are sold everywhere in Belgium. You can get them from a food truck (caravan), fry shacks, or restaurants. We learned about the history of french fries on page 35.

Once you eat french fries from Belgium, you'll want to learn how to make them at home. Here's the secret to Belgian fries:

- They use bintje potatoes (similar to Yukon gold potatoes)
- They are always thick-cut
- They are fried in 100% beef tallow
- They are fried twice. First in a lower heat, then deep fried in a high heat just before serving

Fun Fact: Most Belgians dip their frieten (Dutch) or frites (French) in mayonnaise or "frite sauce."

Mussels

Since the 18th century, mussels have been a staple in Belgian homes. In the wintertime, fish were hard to get, so they collected mussels from the coast of the North Sea.

Today, tourists in Belgium line up for pots of this delicious food. It can be prepared in many different ways, but typically, they are cooked in a white wine sauce, shallots, parsley and butter.

Mussels are popular with a side of french fries. Sometimes, families will order french fries for each person and one pot of mussels to share.

Chocolate!

We learned that chocolate is one of Belgium's largest exports, and its history goes back 4,000 years. You literally cannot go to Belgium without seeing chocolate shops everywhere.

Not only is the quality of chocolate superior in Belgium, but the variety of flavours is like nowhere else on earth.

So, what makes Belgian chocolate so amazing? It starts with the best cocoa beans. Most beans are imported from Africa, mainly the Ivory Coast. Next, Belgians mill the beans so fine that you can't feel any grains on your tongue - it literally melts in your mouth. Belgian chocolate has less sugar than other chocolates because the ingredients like beans and cream are superior.

Fun Fact: Pralines were invented in Belgium. A praline, or Belgian truffle, is a chocolate shell filled with ganache, buttercream, or nut pastes.

Waffles

Try an authentic Belgian waffle if you still have a sweet tooth after all that chocolate.

Technically, waffles were invented in ancient Greece when they poured batter between two irons and cooked it. But the dessert/breakfast dish we love today was created in the Netherlands (before Belgium became its own country) around the 13th or 14th century. In what is now Belgium, people started making something a lot more like our modern waffles but much fancier. The irons had a unique design that would get pressed into the batter. These designs could be anything from a family's coat of arms to beautiful landscapes! When they cooked, they left behind a pattern. These early waffles were often sold outside of churches or at carnivals and fairs.

If you're used to the kind of waffle that goes from the freezer to the toaster, be prepared for a shock! Authentic Belgian waffles are big and fluffy and come with delicious toppings.

Vending Machines (Automaat)

Over the past few years, Belgians have become big fans of rural vending machines. Don't be surprised to see a vending machine in small villages and towns, outside farmers' fields, and next to bakeries.

At the end of the day, when the shops close, instead of bakers throwing out bread, they place the fresh loaves in a vending machine outside their store. This helps their sales and makes it extra convenient for local shoppers.

Many Belgian farmers place a vending machine alongside the road for customers to buy potatoes, apples, strawberries, honey, and even meat!

Vending Machines (Automaat)

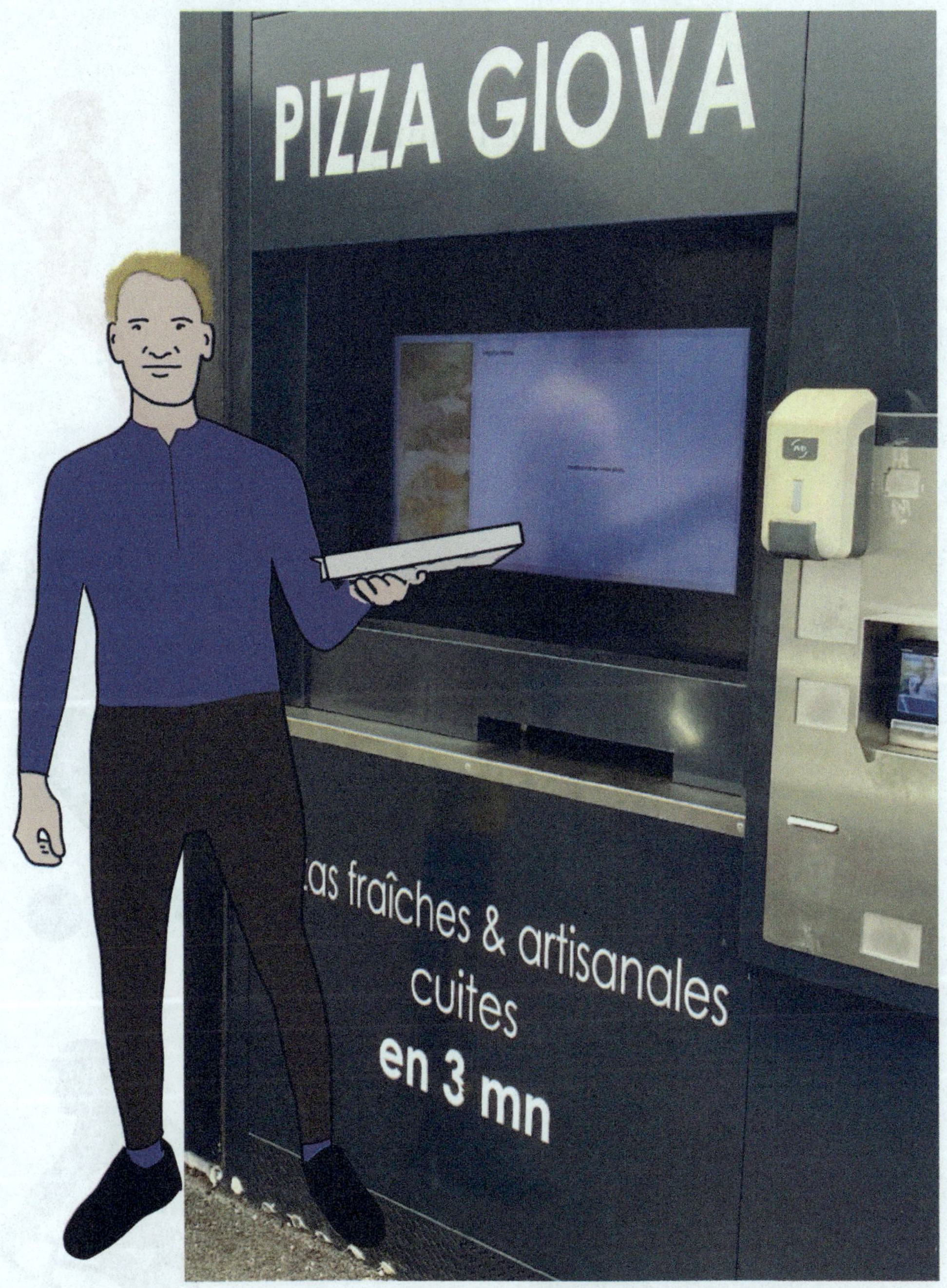

You can even find pizza vending machines in Belgium! Pizzas inside stay at a cool temperature to keep fresh, and once you order one, it goes into a heating chamber and comes out hot in three minutes.

The Most Popular Sports in Belgium

1. Tennis
2. Football (Soccer)
3. Cycling
4. Running
5. Field Hockey
6. Swimming

Krachtbal

Krachtbal, (Flemish for "powerball") originated in Belgium. It's a team sport with four players on each side, including a goalkeeper.

The game is like a cross between basketball, handball and netball with the objective to get the ball into the opposing team's goal.

The ball for krachtbal is a big leather-covered medicine ball weighing up to 4 kg (8.8 pounds). The ball is much lighter for children at 1 kg (2.2 pounds).

There are only two ways to score with the ball: over your head forward for one point, or backward for two points.

Krachtbal is a great game to improve fitness, and no player contact is allowed, making it safe for the players.

Cycling Culture

Cities all over the world are encouraging more people to ride bikes in order to reduce pollution from cars, and to encourage better fitness.

Belgium has a strong bike culture, where many people rely on their bikes for daily commuting to work. With dedicated bike lanes and lots of bike rentals throughout major cities, getting around by bike in Belgium is very popular.

Fun Fact: Antwerp Belgium ranked the 3rd best cycling-friendly city in the world!*

But no country tries harder to make bicycling a fun adventure than Belgium. In the province of Limburg, you can cycle right through a pond! This path in Bokrijk is fast becoming a tourist destination for cyclists. When you are cycling this path, you are at eye-level with the ducks, how fun is that?

You've heard of treetop trekking? Well in Belgium you can go treetop cycling! Cyclists can ride through a double circle bicycle bridge in Bosland, a nature preserve in Limburg. The circled paths climb gradually to the tops of the trees, then circle back down on a gentle slope.

And of course, there is the world-famous championship bike race in Liége (see page 40). So as you can see, Belgians love to cycle!

*Source: Euronews.net June 20, 2023

Cycling in Limburg

Belgian Superstitions

If you rub the head of the Guardhouse Monkey (an iron statue in Mons, Belgium), you will have one year of good luck.

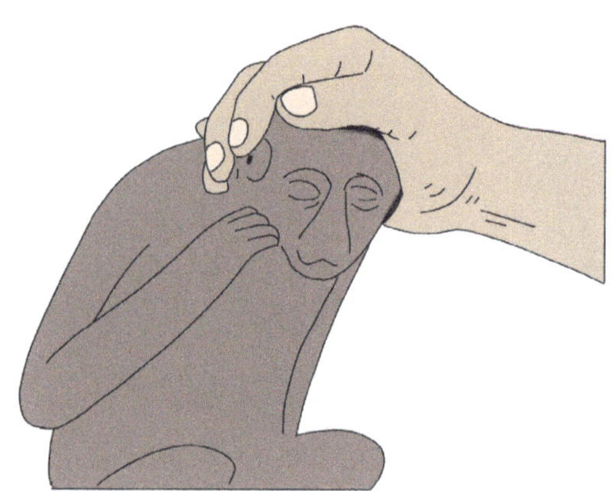

Some Belgian farmers will wish their livestock a happy New Year on January 1 to ensure they stay healthy.

In some countries, Friday the 13th is unlucky. But in Belgium, **Tuesday** the 13th is the unlucky day.

Don't bring poppies into the house or you'll invite lightening strikes.

Funniest Laws in Belgium

Every country has some strange laws still on the books. Belgium is no exception. Although some are no longer enforced, they remain as laws today. Here are some of the strangest:

It is illegal to throw snowballs in Bruges.

You cannot play games or a sport in the vicinity of a church.

In some parts of Belgium it is against the law to hang your laundry outside on a Sunday.

In Ostend, Belgium you are not allowed to bring your cow to the beach between 10:00 a.m. and 7:00 p.m. during tourist season.

Pets in Belgium

Belgians love their pets. In fact, in 2021, 24% of households owned a dog, and 27% owned a cat.

In 2018, it became law in Belgium that a landlord or condo board cannot deny a tenant their right to keep a dog. However, all dogs in Belgium must be microchipped and registered. Also, pets must carry a pet passport in order to travel to another European country. The passport includes health information and verifies its vaccines are up to date.

Cat Parades!

Kattenstoet (Festival of Cats) is held in Ypres, Belgium every three years on the second Sunday in May. This festival has been going on since 1955.

The history of the festival goes back to the middle ages when cats were considered bad luck and related to witchcraft. But today, cats are celebrated by parades with giant floats. The Jester (in the red pointy hat), climbs to the top of the Cloth Hall and tosses cat plushies to the people below.

If you happen to be in Belgium on May 12, 2024, or May 9, 2027, that's when the next parades will be.

Tot Ziens, Au Revoir, Verabschiedung, Goodbye

After learning so much about Belgium, you can understand why it is such a great place to go on holiday. Belgium is steeped in history, the people are warm and friendly, and the food is fantastic. Besides, who couldn't love a country famous for chocolate!

About the Author

Collette is a world-traveller and proud G-Mom to Julien and Beau! She loves to write about travelling and is excited to help inspire others to embrace their inner explorer. Having visited all seven continents, she looks forward to taking her grandsons on some epic adventures one day! They love to request books and contribute new ideas often.

To see more books by Meonatrip, scan the QR code below.

Please leave an honest review on Amazon; it will go a long way to creating more books like this one.

Acknowledgements:

Pg 7 "Rainy Antwerp" by vinmar is licensed under CC BY-SA 2.0.
Pg 8 "Vlissingen - Eunice (storm)" by mauriceweststrate is licensed under CC BY 2.0.
Pg 15 "De Triangel A Freinet Primary School in Booischot Belgium - Hall of the new building Sept 2018" by Sally V is licensed under CC BY-SA 4.0.
Pg 19"Metro station In Brussels Ref-117" by infomatique is licensed under CC BY-SA 2.0.
Pg 18 "The never-used metro of Charleroi" by LHOON is licensed under CC BY-SA 2.0.
Pg 19 "Public transport in Flanders" by MunichTramSpotter is licensed under CC BY 2.0.
Pg 19 "File:DB ICE TRAIN AT BRUSSELS NORD STATION BELGIUM JULY 2012 (7690240942).jpg" by calflier001 is licensed under CC BY-SA 2.0.
Pg 20 "Skods Taxis in Brussels" by Raf24-commonswiki is licensed under CC BY-SA 4.0
Pg 21 "Tilted building and rolling hills along the RAVeL5 L38 in Thimister-Clermont, Belgium (DSCF5974)" by Trougnouf (Benoit Brummer) is licensed under CC BY 4.0.
Pg 21 "L'entrée du chenal (Nieuwpoort Beach -Belgium)" by Flikkersteph -5,000,000 views ,thank you! is licensed under CC BY 2.0.
Pg 22 "Forest Path in the Ardennes" by *rboed* is licensed under CC BY 2.0
Pg 22 "Modern Brussels" by dungodung is licensed under CC BY-SA 2.0.
Pg 24 "File:Leo Belgicus - C.J. Visscher (1650), 6 - BL.jpg" by Creator:J. van Doetechum Creator:C.J. Visscher is marked with CC0 1.0.
Pg 26 "Port scenes, Antwerp" by imo.un is licensed under CC BY 2.0.
Pg 30 "Brussels" by HerryLawford is licensed under CC BY 2.0.
Pg 31 "Inside the Atomium" by o palsson is licensed under CC BY 2.0.
Pg 31 "Mini Europe" by Maria Firsova is licensed under CC BY 2.0.
Pg 32 "OO-SND A320 Brussels Airlines" by markyharky is licensed under CC BY 2.0.
Pg 32 "Belgium. Brussels. Museum of Tintin." by Anne & David (Use Albums) is marked with Public Domain Mark 1.0.
Pg 33 "Canal Tour Boat, Bruges" by Peter K Burian is licensed under CC BY-SA 4.0.

Acknowledgements:

Pg 34 "Choco-Story" by JavaSquid is licensed under CC BY 2.0.
Pg 35 "Frietmuseum" by JavaSquid is licensed under CC BY 2.0.
Pg 35 "Historium Bruges" by Julien Maury is marked with Public Domain Mark 1.0.
Pg 36 "Buitengevel Plopsa Station Antwerp" by Bumba86 is licensed under CC BY 4.0.
Pg 37 "Antwerp Zoo" by Morgaine is licensed under CC BY-SA 2.0.
Pg 37 "Antwerp Zoo" by Nigel Swales - 2 is licensed under CC BY-SA 2.0.
Pg 37 "Antwerp zoo, Belgium" by pelican is licensed under CC BY-SA 2.0.
Pg 38 "Introduction room Ghent City museum STAM" by Phile Deprez is licensed under CC BY-SA 4.0.
Pg 38 "Gravensteen Castle with Moat - Ghent Belgium" by bvi4092 is licensed under CC BY 2.0.
Pg 39 "Dinant y los saxos" by morrissey is licensed under CC BY 2.0.
Pg 40 "Liege-Bastogne-Liege 2019-44" by adrian.betteridge is licensed under CC BY 2.0.
Pg 40 "File:Liege-Bastogne-Liege 2016.png" by Psemdel is licensed under CC BY-SA 4.0.
Pg 40 "Belgian Grand Prix" by Malte Niehuis is licensed under CC BY_SA 3.0.
Pg 41 "File:Comic Con Brussels 2016 - Cosplay Contest (26609616541).jpg" by Miguel Discart from Bruxelles, Belgique is licensed under CC BY-SA 2.0.
Pg 42 "2020-09-20_11-14-49_ILCE-6500_DSC06267_DxO" by miguel.discart is licensed under CC BY-SA 2.0.
Pg 42 "New without information" by RightIndex is licensed under CC BY 2.0.
Pg 42 "Billy The Cat (Colman/Desberg)" by RightIndex is licensed under CC BY 2.0.
Pg 51 "Carnaval de Binche - Mardi Gras" by ines s. is licensed under CC BY 2.0.
Pg 51 "File:Malmedy carnaval Luc Viatour 3.jpg" by Luc Viatour is licensed under CC BY-SA 3.0.
Pg 52 "File:Malmedy carnaval Luc Viatour 5.jpg" by Luc Viatour is licensed under CC BY-SA 3.0.
Pg 52 "The Giants of the North, Dunkirk Carnival" by www.thegoodlifefrance.com is licensed under CC BY 2.0.
Pg 54 "Sinterklaas zwarte piet" by Michell Zappa] is licensed under CC BY-SA 2.0.

Acknowledgements:

Pg 57 "French fries are not from France." by Cristy Valencia is licensed under CC BY 2.0.
Pg 58 "Mussels, mussels restaurant, Brussels, Belgium" by gruntzooki is licensed under CC BY-SA 2.0.
Pg 59 "Belgian chocolate shop" by Jess & Peter Gardner is licensed under CC BY-SA 2.0.
Pg 60 "File:Waffles (Belgium).jpg" by Tamorlan is licensed under CC BY 3.0.
Pg 61 "Nossegem Breadautomat" by Andrew69 is licensed under CC0 Public Domain
Pg 62 "Pizza vending machine near our home in Samrée, Belgium (2022) by MollySVH is licensed under CC BY 2.0
Pg 66 "File:2017 Toerisme Limburg Cycling through Water Cycling path at dawn.jpg" by Visitlimburg.be is licensed under CC BY-SA 4.0.
Pg 70 "The Cat Parade, Ypres" by VISITFLANDERS is licensed under CC BY-NC-ND 2.0.

MEONATRIP

2023

Made in the USA
Coppell, TX
02 March 2025

46594707R00046